I0901379

aphelion

aphelion

Jenna Butler

NeWest Press

Copyright
©
Jenna Butler
2010

All rights reserved. The use of any part of this publication reproduced, transmitted in any form or by any means, electronic, mechanical, recording or otherwise, or stored in a retrieval system, without the prior consent of the publisher is an infringement of the copyright law. In the case of photocopying or other reprographic copying of the material, a licence must be obtained from Access Copyright before proceeding.

Library and Archives Canada Cataloguing in Publication

Butler, Jenna, 1980–
Aphelion / Jenna Butler.

Poems.
ISBN 978-1-897126-60-8
I. Title.

PS8603.U844A65 2010
C811'.6
C2009-906235-6

Editor for the Board:
Douglas Barbour
Cover and interior design:
Natalie Olsen, Kisscut Design
Author photo:
Icon Experience Photography

NeWest Press acknowledges the support of the Canada Council for the Arts, the Alberta Foundation for the Arts, and the Edmonton Arts Council for our publishing program. We also acknowledge the financial support of the Government of Canada through the Book Publishing Industry Development Program (BPIDP).

NEWEST PRESS
201, 8540–109 Street
Edmonton, Alberta T6G 1E6
780.432.9427
www.newestpress.com

No bison were harmed in the making of this book. We are committed to protecting the environment and to the responsible use of natural resources. This book was printed on 100% post-consumer recycled paper.

1 2 3 4 5 13 12 11 10
printed and bound in Canada

For Thomas.

Contents

North America

The solemn & inexhaustible eloquence of rains and mountain.
O the playful heaves and tumble of lines in the hills here.
We are first green and then grey and then nothing in this world.

DENISE RILEY

Heatwave

Stop now. Hold it there. Balance. Be beautiful. Try.
—And I can't do this. I can't talk like any of this.
You hear me not do it.

DENISE RILEY

She almost makes it
through the first week.

They've stacked his boxes
by the curb; one night

it rains, diaphanous sheets,
she knows she should feel glad —

feel something —
but all she can picture is

his set of Vonnegut;
damp pages clinging

like tentative hands.
She wishes now

they'd gotten to Mexico,
stunned into quietude

by bougainvillea's brightness,
conspirators in the mosaicked heat.

Given the choice,
they would travel by train,

fumbling over the stacks of bills
smelling of sweat and a thousand palms;

the small man behind the wicket
sunning, early siesta.

They'd cram the bags
in overhead bins,

old diesel engine panting,
part with nickels for mangoes

and nip back the pungent skin.
Trace the palm lines of hills.

But the rain, now;
that dampens everything

past repairing.
How could she have told him

it's really about
the way light falls in a high room

midsummer, the wind picking out
the scent of lemons and beeswax

from old furniture, the lawn lounging
uncut and insouciant.

The heat is what he doesn't understand —
that, and the way sunlight cuts

whitely through unsashed windows;
how she likes to stand with the glare

refracting over her. Stripping her clean.
Something about

being prismatic.
Asking nothing.

Berrying, Gabriola Island

we follow the scent   blackberries
roped across the headland
panopoly of August fruit

they reach hard canes
into this impossible soil
thrust down fingers
and root   unstring themselves
along cliff edges
spined   taunting

under their canopy
the bruised grass where
deer have gathered
anxious   for windfall

this fruit has been known
to scupper boats
in the Narrows   women
ploughing ashore
sans oars   sans tow line
eyes fixed
on scarab berries

we eat
beneath a rivalry of
late-season wasps
canes bent
to mouths hard and
bright with need

starvelings at
one Tree or another

Arrow Lakes Ferry, 1995

In Memoriam: Nan Norwood

two cars on the late crossing
above the pier   ospreys in blotted kohl
    the perfunctory dives of the merlins
    their malachite eyes

on deck   we eat herb salad
dredged from the morning garden
tarragon and lime
thick curls of basil
with their verdigris sheen

all this undercut by
the winch's semitone hum
inexorable pull
across a skin of water

Granville Island, 1997

dusk condensing   tenebrous
interstitial sweep of shadows
pockmarking brickwork

Madeira shingles the tongue
assuages salt rasp
    blue jazz over a harbour
    traced in lights

stolen minutes
between quarter-tones

certainty of your leaving
brilliant as stars
    white-hot
    above umbels of streetlamps

threat of your absence
unassailable   as the moon
shatters itself
over stones

Sandon

the tenacity of this town
held back the mountains

at night
the swaybacked hills
limned licentious red

    brothels thick with
    cassia   sandalwood

this morning
we negotiate spent slopes
at limping pace

rear tire blown
on gravel   the spare
stuttering like
a second-rate heart

on the western rise
the town crooks in its joints
furls   its old prehensile roadways

expired mineshafts cough
gouts of tailings
    oblivious to the shift of
    itinerant granite

this town undone at last
by a slip of river
nudged free from flume
    silver heft of water beneath the floor

the impeccable certainty that
one must rise
or drown

Homecoming

these are the rivers
of my childhood

we lay
hidden in reeds
on August afternoons
cupping plums
    fragrant blue gems

the roiling eddies
of the Bow
seamed with minnows and
twists of hay
from the homeward pass
of the threshers at dusk

North Saskatchewan
swollen with pack ice
    ragged jigsaw in spring
    gnawing bridge anchors
sluicing away over
the occasional corpse
blank and blue-eyed
embracing the sky

these are the torrents
that thrill in our veins
  that drive us forth
        that carry us home

Winter Highway

november   we descend
from permafrost north
camp on the ice

fire on a bier
above the river
poplar logs   green and sappy
snow pitted from
the flankers' fall

all day   we follow
the trucks gone before
    chancing thin ice
    for tea   white bread
    ten-pound sacks of potatoes

fifty kilometres upriver
men detox on the trap lines
wait   for the trucks to return
for their friends to come through
with rum   with whiskey

all summer
the settlement has sunk into itself
feral   bald-toothed

squatted by the river
squinted blearily into
the hazy sunshine

waited for the ice

Kerouac

his family heaved a sigh of relief
the day he hopped a train
and disappeared from their lives
    at least until the following Christmas

under the trees in the woodlot
his meditation place grew over   threaded with wild blue flax
they mowed it under in September for hay

never a postcard
although once a slip of paper
with lines from Hanshan
which his mother pretended to understand
justifying its place on the mantel

out in the Arizona night
home   a thousand acres of desert sand
shot through with shadows
the Mexicali girls
brought port
danced unafraid by the tracks

woke to his absence
and the dawn cinders of the Express

watched the slow sunlight
enter the imprint of his body
and obliterate his passing

Chilies

summer   you picked
them first thing after sunup
brought them to me   steaming
    the greenhouse wallowing
    at the end of the garden
    some opaque   bereft pearl

those chilies   we devoured
on the seawall where
your house dangled its stilt legs
over the Strait

lime and coarse salt   our lips
insensitive with heat
the cove's soft limbs
clambering up from tideline
    that thin   bright rim
    brushstroked with herons
    their sanguinary calm

and the rinds spangled
with seeds   sucked
to vanishing point
cusp of the bay

hot and shining
    some sort of
    meteor shower   our mouths
scalded into brightness

Ghost Highway (Route 61)

they line
the sides of this road
like touchstones
    worn ropes
    of sunwarmed rock
stubble of towns
landscape punctuated with
clapboard   ravenous willows

    achromatic prairie clarity

somewhere past
the nap and fold of grain
shadow of these towns
in hairline tracery
   buried   perhaps
   under cranesbill
   pungent wormwood

nonetheless   there

Cutline

cold-air crackling
      warming gut
      expanding sinew
ash rackets
confound the drifts

          hieroglyphic
                    sparrowtracks

intervals of paper birch
black and   white
striating winter pines

buckle-kneed deer
betrayed by whiskeyjacks
    ruffled   circling

      wings pressed softly
      against a fretted sky

Salt Spring Island

In Memoriam: Lilo Berliner & Wilson Duff

in your words
a certain   sirocco

brackish   emphatic heat
prelude to vacuum

i come to this knowing
by reading   i acknowledge
your absence   his

the blunt vegetal heft of
these racemes of paper
their importuning tongues

in the meditation garden
Shiva's limbs a dour Esperanto

i begin to see you
less clearly   more truly

Wild Indigo

summer turns her polyglot
down in the dirt amongst
lettuce   trumpet lilies   rosemary
my mother
    resolutely unilingual
suddenly fluent in her mongrel tongue
    demi-resurrection of Latin
    genera   phyla   common names
love-in-a-mist   *campanula*

in her palms
the diurnal breath
of amaranthus   plush ropes
turgid stems
throttling the garden
            vegetative hegemony

confluence
her hands   words
lifting   naming

indigo   rampant and fragile
held to light
dusty blue
like sky or   midwinter stars

Petroglyph Trail

under the trees   the path
falters to bedrock
    ash and chainlink
    salal   a riot of berries

we lick
our fingers   trace
cryptic outlines
knuckle stones where
the lichen gives way

wonder at
this patient sunlight
its citrine crawl

how it obscures
some things   reveals
these others

Letter to Nancy

light catches the stone
just   so
revealing hairline fractures
small imperfections

we did not notice you
slipping into the spaces
between the leaves
   creasing yourself
   between pavement slabs
running   through our fingers

      this granite
      an astonishment

we did not expect
the sudden fall
of empty   light

the trampled grass
and muffled soil

dusk breaking
across marble
      reconfiguring
      your absence

Habbakuk

The Ice Ship

they cut it free for the first time
that spring the firs
shorn back from water
like scissored pelt

all winter they had cobbled it
from lake ice nacred slabs
dappled with wood pulp
hand-hewn and
meshing with the glide of bone

on the bank amidst
February's leavings
    alders knotted with
    high-tension cables
    oil like abalone in pale sun
the workers watched
Churchill's brainchild breach and hold

but ice is just
another word for romance
to those who have never known
the glassine cold of winter

when the camps had gone
    cinderblocks tumbled and
    seamed with spruce
the ice ship melted on
a dark pout of lakeshore
and the rind of a war
ended too far
too soon

Blueberry Season

In Memoriam: Jack White Goose Flying (d. 1899)

before the road came
a hasty grave   buckthorn marker
one less boy going north come spring
inured to the residential school
its polymorphous Christ

in the basin of June heat   his family
read the cracked pan of floodplain
took their remaining children
turned home

the grave accreted
in the way of recondite things
a picket fence   whitewashed
some sort of story

all of it   eventually
hamstrung by highway
the school down to fragments   his bones
sharp and thin
as serried wheat

and come summer   the blueberry bushes
a density of fresh red canes
as after flooding
or a deeprooted burn

Red Deer River Valley

These rocks release, at dusk,
the latent heat of a Jurassic sun,

suffusing the canyons with the scent of sage,
crushed juniper, wild pea vine.

Out in the musky dark, Coyote sings
the praises of an August night in reedy treble,

the distant buzz of his trickster's rattle
under the stones, the breathless weight

of shadow crouching inscrutable
below moonbleached plateau.

A thousand years ago, they slipped the traces
off dogs and women, descended through

opalescent June nights
to the cottonwoods by the river.

These stones have seen the dancing
by firelight, the careful weave

of quills and doeskin,
deepthroat resonance of drums.

They hold the fleeting glimpse of
morning on a dusty stretch of ground

picked out in stone circles,
the slow-beating wings of proprietary hawks.

In a dry-rock crevice, a child's grave.
A tuft of fur, buckskin blanket. One crimson feather.

(Native) Land

I.

we walk two worlds
you and i

hitched up against
borders
  rubbed raw
  by intention

there is no language
for the sidelined tongue

our words
are the smoke
of cookfires
falling on blue evening
when all else sleeps

II.

do not come
with woodsmoke in your hair
redolent of earth
and silence

they do not want
your handful of stories
the ochre touch
of your palm

Coming Home After Rain

I.

across the bay   trawlers picked out in lights
fishermen setting their night lines

the sandstone here undercut into waves
sea just out of reach

on the north road   old pines
thinned to copse   windbreak

what it means to bend
the dim   soft curve of horizon

silent house   but
the porch lamp on

II.

this brittle sound   seabreeze
the marram grass in spite of itself

draw of sea on shingle   pipers
knotted amongst the stones

drydock   two sloops butterflied
bow to stern

up from the government wharf
a gauntlet of cormorants

night wind in the rigging
coming home after rain

Inter-Tribal

Songhees Powwow, 2003

the ravens come first
angle over the men as they
mow out the dancing circle
strut black and curious
through the cuttings

the trucks racket in
like wagons cruise
the hills for tenting space

dusk and
the arena lights
reach up long poles
wires gathered in loops bundled
behind stalls selling
bannock tooled leather

fancy dancers
crooked into motion
arms wide jingle cones
swing and chime
the grandmothers stately
in shawls newly-beaded doeskin
  five hundred hours of
  double-stitch by lamplight

i dance
the thin red soil of Dodoma
peach trees jasmine
bitter lengths of coffee farms
strung along irrigation ditches
the rich bronze sun

Tanzania razed by civil war
lopped off at   the roots

we dance   what holds us
sustains us   sends us on
the light falls fallow   the high pines
ascend into blue air
rigged with smoke

a gleaming rind of moon
and the ravens
part of the deeper dark

Jazz

For George Szirtes

The sound of a city
jumped up on oil money,
tail end of the Boom;
the eighties reeking of
leather and Naugahyde,
self-important bloom of
Capitalism in love with
its own reflection.
In Toronto, my mother watched
her family scatter over
two continents, an ocean;
waited, as one accustomed,
for her father's death, for
her husband's summons.

This music permeates
twenty years. The winters grew
ragged; the searing air that
wrapped the houses carried
the scent of woodsmoke. Blue guitar
underwrote the evenings. Older,
returning from bars in dim, grey hours,
a soft sax riff thrilled through the streets;
we crept to bed pursued by music;
that fleeting harmony.

Perhaps this is why my fingers stumble;
they've learned the keys,
which cadence calls on sudden joy,
arpeggiated crests; the falls
of light and mood this music brings.
But more than that — the rhythm holds
a rich, dark frame; chords weave
and cling. The sound of loss,
of bearings gained
reluctantly; above the buckle,
toss of time, its scope
the heart's estranged melody.

Weather

There is in this world one snow fall.
Everything else is just weather.
MATTHEW HOLLIS

I.

Saskatoon. Chokecherry. Those
stained fingers. Incarnadine days.

Snow geese on a curl of slough,
massed water seething.

In spite of rain, space for two:
ornamental plum, its blowsy skirts.

A man's garden. Syrian tobacco,
hibiscus straining against trellis.

What this is not. A game. Later:
anything but easy.

2.
From Amisk, the hills unfurl
west into rainshadow.

Iron arc of pain across scapula. How
birds are tugged to flight.

Mattock awry by the toolshed door.
Loss like ozone, sulky blue.

What she said & what we felt
never locked eyes; that sideslip gaze.

Your absence is a little death.
Heart pocketed, fumbled smooth.

3.
Patience & what it means: November,
rainwater turning glass.

Midafternoon sun in the conservatory.
Monarch's slow battery against the panes.

Her words: *or else.* In the garden,
sleet needles into turf.

Duplicity not our own:
an early snow. Songbirds gone.

Cold-air peal of axe in beech.
The coppice wracked & bare.

4.
An imperfect control.
Love, migration. All manner of flight.

Unasked: windflowers
crowding the doorstep.

Scythed out from orchard grass.
One fox, running umber.

Panacea for the unexpected:
hot, sweet tea.

Ridgeline trail, the scent of juniper.
Thrill of edge & over.

5.
Gaps like afterimage. These
mementoes we cannot help but keep.

Opposite ends of the same room
thinking, *thunder.*

Amaryllis in thick brocade;
strictures of the season.

Balsam fir. Forced bulbs: pink.
Hyacinths' harlot bloom.

Do not do this. Your
caged-bird look. Hands limp behind glass.

6.
Not *because* of you;
in spite of. Love, spring.

Titanium. Cimmerian. White,
ways of saying.

If not this, then.
What? Fearing stasis.

Overnight, freezing rain.
The alders gleaming, transfixed.

Late juncos. After-storm light.
Among others, not ours to keep.

7.
Loss in this moment:
dogwood blooms against frost.

No, but gently. In the dooryard,
wisteria jags across eaves.

How not like snow —
name for every state of being.

Me you / I;
limpwristed voice trailing after.

Every place war has left —
what you cannot return to.

8.

To avoid disaster, less auspicious fruit.
(Eve, Atalanta.)

Sound against sound, this end of season.
Autumn's gunmetal hum.

Lifetime in this hour or that.
We hold like mayflies; love fast.

Wild lupine, checkerspot: to live
with so little, such brilliance.

The Battlefords have their claws in you.
Song for the solstice; auroraed night.

9.

Antimony spring; the cowslips
bend, break with nectar.

Months without word. Sea
lips in, in, away.

History's copper road:
sitka, cedar at twilight.

We said we would not
be here again. Sky goes alum, clay.

Wren arcs through, intent on air,
thimble-shift of bones.

10.

Not what, but how.
Spring. You — and not you.

Moonscape in the woodlot grass;
clavicle pooled with rain.

Defy these odds:
hoarfrost & cherry blossom.

On the phone: surf.
Noises of return.

Early swarm transfigures the orchard.
Synchronicity: light on wings.

11.

In the muskeg spruce, one raven,
plumdark and shrieking.

Say, *home*. Say, *I am*.
Convince me.

Dubious bloom: cinnamon bear
amongst birch.

The new aspen grove laid low
overnight. Wind & heart rot.

Starvation winter:
a consciousness of bone.

12.

Surviving the first night alone —
that you do not break when dawn does.

Living so close & not meeting takes
luck. A certain resolution.

Green heartwood rimed with ice;
bur oaks shatter under sleet.

Pine siskin, chickadee.
Cardinal a vague, occasional flame.

Wild oats lean toward
winter. Longing & loss.

Europe

World is crazier and more of it than we think,
Incorrigibly plural. I peel and portion
A tangerine and spit the pips and feel
The drunkenness of things being various.

LOUIS MACNEICE

Mercury's Gift

She keeps joss sticks in a japanned wooden box
smelling faintly of hyssop

and grease, the bold strokes of the craftsman's blade,
the curls of cedar falling.

She airs the room out after the old man has gone,
his musky scent fading to adumbration,

tucks hyacinths into a frosted vase,
fragrance attenuating the early air.

Thousands of years from now,
women will talk amongst themselves

of this moment, rolling her name
across their tongues like rue;

such balm in the leaves,
such latent poison.

He ought to have known her better,
the physiognomy of betrayal.

In her lambent eyes,
the mutter of boxed-in wings.

Little Boy Blue

two a.m.
sickle moon limelighting windowpanes
clawing ineffectually through alleys

slam of billiard balls
socketed away like joints
miasma of cigarettes
whiskey sours

you
backlit with pool cue

in the morning
will scramble eggs
slap on Gorecki
run your wife a bath
retreat in the steam

fumble over answers

Miscarriage, First Trimester

this furnace, this fire
in a corner of the body's dark

this is the place that burns
whatever has been broken

STEVEN MICHAEL BERZENSKY

there must be some way   she thinks
of naming this
of finding the language
to anneal the body   its losses

peelings   she will say
to a physician disinclined
to visualization   *filaments*
and in a moment of inspiration   *polyps*
feathered   *arborescent*

picturing the last miniature forests
bordering the Marianas   a luminous sweep
encircling submarine vents
one last shimmer over
the long exhale into dark

Demeter, After

She fumbles with the spoon,
scattering gemmed kernels;

too impatient, always;
now this humiliation.

Her chapped lips snap at the fruit.
Mother, people have given up worlds

for pomegranates; ripe red seeds
stripped from their pouches

at the wrong time, in darkness —
a thick voice sudden in the ear.

The mothers stand on the bank,
hands full of grain, the chaff of it,

praying to where the earth opened and
swallowed their daughters down.

It cannot be like this —
the mothers withering,

unable to do anything but
sit by the cave, tuning the lute.

The ones left behind
do not do this; crave the seeds,

sit uncomprehending. They go out,
find jobs. Lovers. They buy flowers,

decorate the earth yearly
with lilies, pungent rue.

This is where the daughters vanished.
This is where we went to ground.

Aphelion

the light
mealy   seven o'clock
preluding Mediterranean clarity

under the palms
the men deal cards
chew cumin seeds   your absence
outlined against the day

i recall
your gaze   alembic
my body
condensing into flesh
across the table

Keswick

the light here just off true
eyes blurred by cloud by distance

what opens flint-riddled hills
church cradled like balm

bridle path cutting into dusk
rank and white with hawthorn

the rookery a cuckoo
borrows dark wings

cow parsley shatters into bloom
our grief in the forgetting

Returnings

when we have gone too far
memory   like cairns
tumbled pebbles
remember this   bring stones

night elegy in the scuttling blackbirds

remembrance   is in the wings
between the bones
their avian heft or
the chimeric flight
of bumblebees

rooks like soot along the church fence
what you said   *come home*

under the horse chestnut
two young boys pass
a cigarette   blossom
in their hands
fragrant   fragmentary

Versailles

at her demand
the tulips surrender
their succulent heads

she plows barefoot
through thyme
golden oregano
    creases the gazing pool
    with scented instep
cardinals
criticize her progress
from the black walnut

the long hall
brilliant with light
in early morning
    caged finches silent

Marie
                        in a mirror

                                    in a mirror

Stained Glass

your beauty

bombed-out
like Reims
   the rose windows
   torn from lead sockets
            scattered over   snow

and i
shine through
your empty places
           gaptoothed intervals of dark

not so much
the presence of light
but the sudden lifting
of shadow

Mojacar Pueblo

this village that clings
to the lap of hills
a coquettish girl   you
and I   our boots
in these sullen morning streets

outside the bodega
its bitter tint of copal and lemon oil

we drink wine from
bottles of cloudy glass   sound out
the length and breadth of alleyways
with shouts   with song

these old haciendas
ratcheted to their knees
by wild lavender

and beyond them   the sea

Djinat-al-Arif

This morning in the garden I gathered roses,
Fearing the gardener would see me.
Then I heard him gently say:
'You only want flowers? I give you the whole garden.'
JALAL-UD-DIN RUMI

Bustan, Garden of Flavours

Under the shade trees
the children hunt for limes,
crush the sour green rinds
for juice, lick stinging palms.
The gardener knocks the sluices
with a stone crock, hauls them free
to stack, dripping, on the terrace;
measures the limpid artery of
water creeping beneath the hedges.
Two days past the citrus harvest;
the last bergamots in shrunken skins,
paper casings of blossom
skim the fountains, swag
the paving stones in creped petals.
Beneath the medlars, two old men
drag their feet, chew cumin;
the bittersweet tang
of endings, of autumn. Deride
the thin slanting rain that
scours the flesh raw,
ripens and rots everything
fragrantly, to the core.

Gulistan, Garden of Fragrance

The sun teases petals
from the Judas trees, the air
redolent with spices; pepper,
alyssum. The gazing ponds shelter
a tread-worn stair. Beneath
the cypresses, each frond of
fiddlehead, birch, bittersweet
an evocation. This land
says *stay*; the scent of banksia rose
the same that met the Nasrid kings
along these paths. The very beams
that form the gates are oiled and hung
with jasmine, cream upon the lathes,
the dubious moulded plaster.
This garden's scent is history.
Around the slumped and rotting walls,
the terraces, the limber halls
eclipsed by light, it moves and breathes.
Throughout the lengthy summer dusk,
the rain-washed leaves and subtle tang of
evening stock make sweetly plain:
the garden continues without us.

Riyad, Garden of Music

This is a place to linger. All hours,
the palace workers come and go;
from task to task, to lilting tones
of fountains, flowing water. The women gather
with silken thread to knot the posies:
jasmine blossom, pink and red
valerian. To cut this strand,
the garden bursts forth in sudden bloom
upon the table, the open hand.

Mundham Common Road

this morning
we split the early clouds
inclined   above Dover

brief glimpse
eclipsed by tailings of high mist

tonight
the cart-track runs on unchanged
signpost to the Common
bucked up on its disintegrating plinth

        scent of lavender

it is as if
the road holds the memory
of our footsteps
the fallow recalls
the hunger of our eyes in passing
and our hands
parting the grass for sorrel
    bitter on the tongue
    so late in the season

the light opens again
those images
we once devoured

forgetting to feel
fearing only
dim recall
        symptom of distance

forgetting
that this land
not only appears
but evokes

  not only seems
  but breathes

Prometheus

I.

soldiers found his wife
amid whorls of jasmine

in the kitchen garden   the acacias
reeking   dank with gum

her luminous gaze
distracted   nascent understanding

caught by
westward semaphore

  morning's prescient
  crop of crows

II.

what he must have thought
of   us

    suspended in abattoir glow
      june dawn

still point in
a centrifuge of eagles

even then
we would not look up

in the end   only Cassiopeia
her rope of stars

Michaelmas

Whatever there is in me
that is singing,
whatever there is in me,

you are there too
DI BRANDT

rain pelts down
nine o clock   and september
and you   five thousand miles away
over water

i trace droplets down doubleglaze
stark against miasma of streetlamps

perhaps where you are   it is bright
and crisp   early winter   blue
you cannot feel
the slap and glide of
drizzledamp wool

smell the heady fug
of bonfires left
unturned and smouldering
twists of oak leaves
cindering slow
   ponderous opalescent smoke

but i imagine
you   on the porch   attuned
to the harping of coyotes
out on the ice

ululation moving through you
cool and tenuous as rain

The Red Ghazals

Speak
steadily as is needed to
stare down beauty. That calms it.

DENISE RILEY

I.

morning smog   stitched with pigeons
sky seeded in afterbirth light

she puts on coffee   adds liquor
these old cups warming to our hands

huddled on the couch   wakeful
staring down your empty house

what to do with   this
inherited   miscellany

trying to jigsaw a pattern
around your sudden absence

2.

the moment after you leave
and i   cannot

returning to finger   sheets
pillowcases   redolent of your hair

my inability to disconnect   as you do
this life from my other

your departure
coalescing into sound

sudden silence after train's passing
implosion   blood against inner ear

3.

snow geese in solstice passage
wingbeats to gypsy tempo of sun

instinct   awakened
from dormancy

flock etched flat
against spring density of blue

rolling down from foothills
errantly   on chinook

brilliant
hung like   summer   in suspension

4.

eager hands
strip away   wrappings

caress seductively
finger   bindings

covert inhalation
of   untouched   scent

practiced grip
broken   spine

consecrated death
new page edges under   paperknife

5.

she traverses the halls
on an ecliptic

momentarily negating   all those
in her shadow

she does not speak
unwilling   not unable

pilots the house
by teatime manifesto

blot of raspberry   damask cloth
slow outward crawl of epicentre

6.

striated with triumphant scratches
cottagers' children return from berrying

emerge from thickets   like waxwings
pungent with underbrush

purple with   labour   late August juice
redolent of ferns   pine

drunk and drowsy as bees
at a floral bacchanal

carrying the season
in the vine-ripened tint of their skin

7.

what you do not know   my womb
fisted and nacreous

rumpled cockles   reminiscent of bivalve
unable to open

knowledge like   cherries
glistening   tart

we will never be more than
what we are

what is this   then   but practiced deceit
love conducted like business   over wine

8.

circumscribed in   mundane
your mother   adept at self-effacing

bruises sedimented under makeup
capitulation   for the children

what excuses do you tell   yourself
what   styptic fiction

children treading   littoral borders
omnipresent fear of drowning

mallet retrieved from tool shed
shattered masculine   dominance

9.

your entrance   tentative
bowed under Capuchin scarves

three hours after midnight
my kitchen serving only coffee   black

immediate capitulation
my gaze   caffeinated   condensed

you stumble over reasons   excuses
discarding layers with impunity

all the grace of Penelope
ambushed at midnight   shredding the weft

10.

drawn from fireside   midwinter
summoned by sight of your falling

small imprint etched in feather-oil
traced   on the pane

outside   momentarily stunned
snowbank spattered persimmon

you curl against my fingers   angular
feet recalcitrant   gnarling like twigs

in your eyes   me
behind   glass

II.

yesterday   you slumped
on the street corner   one hip thrust

out   tiredly lascivious
greasy hair shining

in the sun   spitting in the wake
of cars that did not stop

who was it   then   that called you over
sometime after midnight

the next day they find you   spreadeagled
blue glass bottle in your shattered sacrum   glowing

12.

how you can   disassemble   a woman
at the water cooler   over break

mooning against the partition wall
with such   élan

while she   the brunt of your remarks
pretends not to hear

sips from styrofoam   catches your eye
dares you   deeper

she too harbours   dust   bones
she too has secrets

13.

neutral territory   tea house
winter tippling into spring

a girl with bright eyes   hands scented with bergamot
passes us mugs   decrepit stoneware

music undermining the silence   tchaikovsky
whom I never play   because you did

you have taken on a bachelor's patina
poetry books   shabby ones   stubbled chin

this reductive sunlight
blinds   rather than clarifies

14.

the body's ebullience
strung out   the room

redolent with disinfectant
diluvial marble   red on white

she   strung between
bedrails and dialysis

deliquescent flesh
puddling under scalpel lines

womb's
ragged   emphysema

15.

midwinter incongruity
backhoe   among cedars

blue clay
obscured by snow

how one child stands   solemn
while the other   goes to ground

your daughter
hair   brindled with sleet

seeds the slush
with crocus corms

16.

just off the night shift
unpacking fruit

fingertips furred from
peach skin   okanagan

he fell asleep at the wheel
drifted into   oncoming traffic

all I could think of   later
the family in the car he missed

watching him explode against the barricade
like some sort of   star

17.

as children she gave us paan
fragrant with betel spices

we chewed laughed at each other
sticky leaves ringing our mouths red

somehow we never asked our mother
what she was thinking

the betel nut pressed against her tongue
silent as we licked the paan wrappings

taste of home
fading from her lips

18.

bindweed took over the field   behind the house
the summer she was diagnosed

she waged a one-woman vendetta
abandoning garden fork   for butylene torch

he watched her   from the window
incinerating purple blossoms

hungry flame
vapourizing green cartilage

knowing   she could not reach the roots
satisfying herself with eradicating symptoms

19.

the twist of time
wrenching irony of it

that I am here in the breezeway
watching Catalan boats race in the bay

Moroccan tile warming to the sun
thick flesh-toned stucco

that you should miss all this
simply because it comes one year too late

what solace then in the day
in the saffron heat of it

20.

they called it   Widowmaker
not the miners   their wives

sleekly figured   air-pressure driven
two men to hold and one to drill

lungs slowly filling with
rock flour   vessels concretizing

up and down the tunnels
rampant with firedamp

here and there   a trinity exploding
in   momentary   light

21.

semaphoric hawks
against density of blue

farmhouses bare
wind-flagellated siding

reproachful eyes
pellucid   pinioned by shutters

past the creek
mahogany with silt   fermenting leaves

a lone cottonwood extends
bark-shingled pennons

22.

in the morning
they take us to the silk factory

squalid brick
dumpy despite   chasings of sun

cocoons coat the racks
bolts of pilfered silk   secreted in corners

pungent mulch of
tattered mulberry leaves

between workers and worms
a lingua franca of   wings

23.

he knows the warp and heft of wood
its planes and angles

dredged from the bay black walnut
oak sinkers cut loose from log booms

he counts the years
their rings have missed

runs his fingers along livid grain
where current rode back the bark

senses the despair of slipping
beneath waves that came and kept on coming

24.

he panders to the morning crowd
sugared ices   chutney and dahl

wife pinches saffron from
enameled boxes   jewellike stamens

saried daughter mixes semolina for sirro
watches the tourists   watching her

licks the spoon
with languorous tongue

mother   scrutinizes the men's departure
knowing her daughter   follows

25.

the grandmothers have been here since morning
perusing the aisles   abrasive glares

wearing the polish from   woodwork
estate sales in their own futures

absolving them of curiosity
sniping   at the salesgirls

who know nothing about   Chippendale
or this   cenotaphic clutter

    might have been silver
    might have been   gold

26.

that year   the cicadas were
tough as hardtack underfoot

father gave us pennies
to stomp on them   drop the corpses

into the fire   he kept an oil drum alight
for just that purpose

through the fall   i remember
waking at night in sweats

flankers from the drum   hitting the windowpane
soft as   wings

27.

pelleted sleet   scudding
through cutlines

riffing amongst
aeolian birches

sun cups the bank
treacle   opiate

listless in the copse
drugged beyond orbit

november's
abacus of   crows

28.

six hundred kilometres north
he misses the wheatfields   home   her

drinks sloe gin on the veranda at dusk
thinks he can still see the crossbuck

pinwheeling limply in the train's wake
signal-box lights gutted   again

recalls decadent bees
drunk in stonecrop along the rail bed

even here   refusing to change
the cartography of memory

Notes

"Winter Highway": In many areas of northern Canada, the land is too boggy during the summer season to hold a road. Apart from supply drops from small aircrafts, a number of settlements are completely cut off from the outside world during the summer months. Only during the winter, with the freezing of the rivers, do these settlements become accessible — by the so-called "winter highways."

"Salt Spring Island": Lilo Berliner was a librarian at the University of Victoria; Wilson Duff a professor of Anthropology at the University of British Columbia. Although the two had never met, they developed a deep bond through their correspondence and their shared fascination with West Coast Native culture and artifacts. Duff committed suicide by shooting himself in his office, and Berliner, apparently in response to his death, later killed herself by walking into the ocean. Before she died, she left her correspondence with Duff in a package on friend and poet Phyllis Webb's doorstep.

"Habbakuk": The ice ship known as Habbakuk was built by Mennonite prisoners at Patricia Lake in Jasper, Alberta during the Second World War. One of Churchill's romantic war dreams, the ship was to be a prototype of future reinforced iceberg-type aircraft carriers that would help to lay waste to the German U-boats ravaging England's fleet in the Atlantic. By the time Habbakuk neared completion, however, more practical aircraft carriers had been designed for the war effort. Habbakuk was allowed to melt into the waters of the lake, where its wooden framework can be seen to this day.

"Djinat-al-Arif": Original Moorish name of the Generalife gardens in Granada, Spain.

Acknowledgements

Several of these poems have appeared or are forthcoming in the following: *Pandora's Collective, In the Laughter of Stones, Nthposition, Jones Av., Otherwheres, CBC Alberta Anthology, The T.S. Review, The Moosehead Anthology X: Future Welcome, String to Bow, Grain, Writing the Land: Alberta Through Its Poets, Eyewear* and *CV2*. "Weather" appeared as a chapbook from red nettle press.

Much appreciation to the wonderful folk at NeWest Press — Lou, Tiffany, Andy, Loretta, Diane, and Natalie — for making the first book process a really enjoyable one!

Thanks also to Douglas Barbour, for his enduring friendship and support; George Szirtes, for putting up with a fistful of homesick Canadians; and Denise Riley, for wry good humour and advice.

Jenna Butler was born in Norwich, England, close to the North Sea. Her family emigrated to Canada in the early eighties, initially moving to Toronto and finally settling in Alberta. The sense of belonging to, and simultaneously not quite fitting into, two places — England and Canada — has heavily influenced her work, which often focuses on the varied landscapes of these two countries.

Butler holds Bachelor of Arts and Bachelor of Education degrees from the University of Alberta, in addition to a Master's degree in Creative Writing: Poetry from the University of East Anglia. She is currently immersed in her Doctorate of Philosophy from UEA under the supervision of contemporary British poet Denise Riley. She also runs her own poetry house, Rubicon Press, and teaches English at Grant MacEwan University in Edmonton, Alberta.